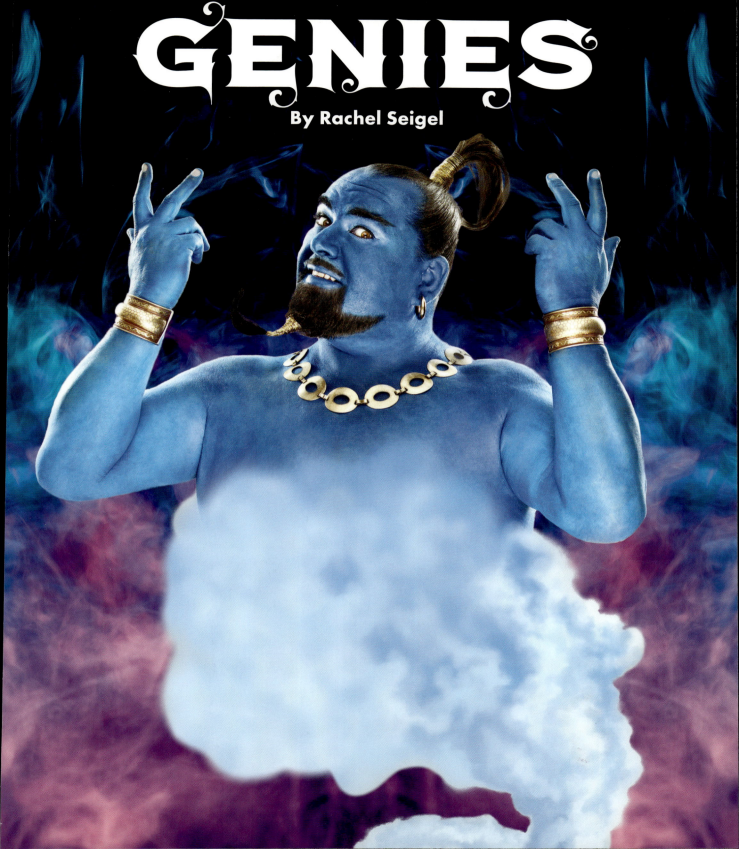

Published by The Child's World®
1980 Lookout Drive • Mankato, MN 56003-1705
800-599-READ • www.childsworld.com

Photographs ©: iStockphoto, cover (genie), 1 (genie), 10, 20; Shutterstock Images, cover (background), 1–3 (background), 9, 13, 14, 23; Anton Ivanov/Shutterstock Images, 5; Romolo Tavani/Shutterstock Images, 6–7, 24; Sarunyu L./Shutterstock Images, 16; Screen Gems/Album/Newscom, 17; Lev Radin/Shutterstock Images, 18; Eugene Gologursky/Getty Images for Macy's, Inc./Getty Images Entertainment/Getty Images, 19

Copyright © 2022 by The Child's World®
All rights reserved. No part of this book may be reproduced or utilized in any form or by any means without written permission from the publisher.

ISBN 9781503849815 (Reinforced Library Binding)
ISBN 9781503850781 (Portable Document Format)
ISBN 9781503851542 (Online Multi-user eBook)
LCCN 2021939351

Printed in the United States of America

Table of CONTENTS

CHAPTER ONE
Looking for Genies...4

CHAPTER TWO
History of Genies...8

CHAPTER THREE
Lamps and Smoke...12

CHAPTER FOUR
Genies Today...16

Glossary...22

To Learn More...23

Index...24

CHAPTER ONE

LOOKING FOR GENIES

Today was a special day. Janna and her family were visiting Jordan, a country in the Middle East. They were going to be **archaeologists** for the day. They would be digging in the city of Jerash. This city was known as Gerasa in **ancient** times. It was thousands of years old. Janna knew that many important **artifacts** had been discovered there. She could not wait to start digging. She wanted to know whether the city had treasure like there was in *Aladdin*.

Jerash is an ancient city in Jordan. It is a popular tourist destination.

Soon they reached the spot where they would dig. The tour guide explained how to use the tools. They got to work. Suddenly, Janna's shovel hit something hard. "I found something!" she shouted. She started brushing away the dirt. The object was smooth.

Legends say that genies live inside magic lamps.

It looked a little like a teapot. She had discovered an old oil lamp. It was just like the kind genies were supposed to live in. Janna knew that genies were not real. But finding the lamp was still exciting. It was fun to imagine what her three wishes would be if there were a genie inside.

CHAPTER TWO
HISTORY OF GENIES

Genies are **supernatural** creatures who are said to have magical powers. Legends of genies can be found in stories that date back to the 600s and earlier. These stories mostly come from countries in the Middle East. Countries in the Middle East include Jordan, Iraq, Yemen, and Saudi Arabia.

People have told stories about jinn *and genies for more than a thousand years.*

The legends talk about supernatural creatures called *jinn*. Some people say that a *jinni* is a spirit. These spirits can be good or evil. They can take many forms. They are also **mischievous**. They have magical powers. *Jinn* are a part of Islam. They appear in the Quran. This is the Muslim holy book. Muslim communities might blame a *jinni* for illness or misfortune. *Jinn* remain a part of the Islamic religion.

Aladdin and the Wonderful Lamp *became popular in Europe after Antoine Galland added it to* The Thousand and One Nights.

Jinn were introduced to other cultures through stories. The most famous story is *Aladdin and the Wonderful Lamp.* This story was originally set in China. A French **translator** named Antoine Galland first heard the story in 1709. A Syrian traveler named Hanna Diyab told Galland the story. Galland translated it. He added it to an Arabic story collection. The collection was called *The Thousand and One Nights.* The word *jinni* became *génie. Génie* is the French word for "genius." Westerners began to form new ideas of genies.

CHAPTER THREE
LAMPS AND SMOKE

Stories about how genies look and behave have changed over time. The genies described in *The Thousand and One Nights* were either invisible or looked human. They could also take any shape. In other stories, the genie appears as a very large man in a robe. In many modern stories, genies have human or half-human bodies. They appear in a puff of smoke. Most genies in Western stories are male. But there have been female genies in television, movies, and comics.

Some genies are tricksters. People must be careful when making wishes.

Many stories say genies become trapped in objects. These can include bottles or lamps. A human usually releases the genie by rubbing the object. Whoever frees the genie gets to make three wishes. But making wishes is not as easy as it sounds. In many legends, genies can trick humans. The genie will follow the exact words of the wish. But the genie can twist the words to hurt the person making the wish. For example, a person could wish to be somewhere warm. The genie might put the person inside a volcano!

Not all stories show tricky genies. Some genies are kind. But they may also have limits to what they can do. Some stories say genies cannot make people fall in love. They cannot bring people back from the dead.

CHAPTER FOUR
GENIES TODAY

Genies often appear as characters in comics, books, movies, and video games. *I Dream of Jeannie* was released in 1965. It was one of the first Western television shows about a genie. The main character is an astronaut. He finds a genie in a bottle after crashing on an island. The genie, named Jeannie, follows the astronaut home.

One of the most famous genies is from Disney's *Aladdin*. The genie is blue. He is a funny and helpful character. The Disney genie wears cuffs around his wrists. These show that he is trapped by the lamp.

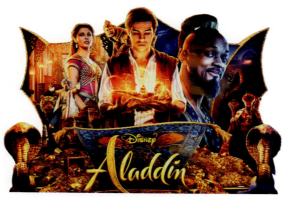

Disney released a live-action version of Aladdin *in 2019.*

Barbara Eden plays Jeannie in I Dream of Jeannie.

Another genie movie is *Kazaam*. It stars basketball player Shaquille O'Neal. He plays a rapping genie who lives in a **boom box**. He grants three wishes to the boy who frees him.

Shaquille O'Neal is best known as a basketball player. But he has acted in many movies and TV shows.

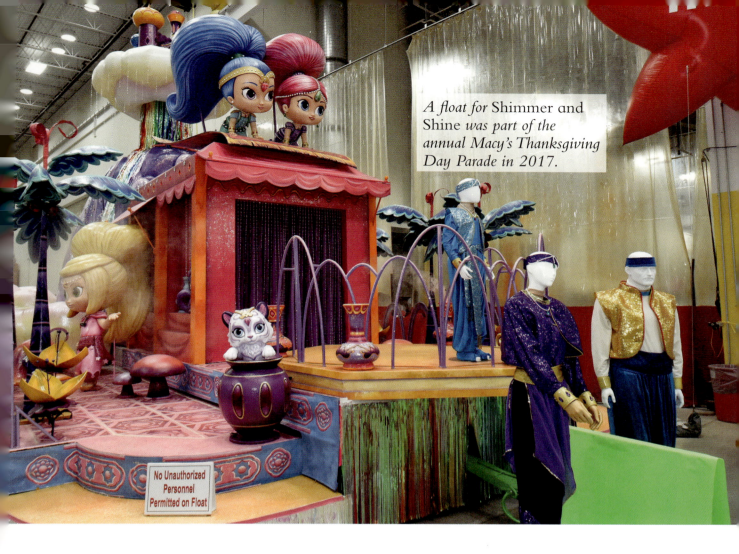

A float for Shimmer and Shine *was part of the annual Macy's Thanksgiving Day Parade in 2017.*

The Nick Jr. cartoon *Shimmer and Shine* is another genie show. It follows the magical adventures of twin genies named Shimmer and Shine. They appear when their human friend Leah rubs her oil lamp necklace. The twins grant three wishes for Leah. But they usually make a mess.

Ma'aruf the Cobbler and his Wife *is another genie story from* The Thousand and One Nights. *People around the world continue to be enchanted by stories of genies.*

In Arabic-speaking countries, genies appear in every issue of the educational children's magazine *Majid.* The magazine uses an illustration of a genie rising from a lamp and giving a computer to an excited boy. The magazine also features traditional folktales that include genies. *Alaa El Din* is another Arabic magazine that features genies. The magazine has a comic strip about the adventures of a modern Aladdin and his genie, Morgan.

Stories of genies have been around for thousands of years. Over time, legends about genies have changed. Genies remain popular in television shows and movies today.

GLOSSARY

ancient (AYN-shunt) Something that is ancient comes from long in the past. Jerash is an ancient city in Jordan.

archaeologists (ar-kee-AW-luh-jists) Archaeologists are scientists who study objects that people from the past left behind. Archaeologists work with special tools to protect and save the objects they find.

artifacts (AR-tuh-fakts) Artifacts are human-made objects, such as tools, that are related to past life and human activities. Many artifacts from ancient people can be found in museums.

boom box (BOOM BAHKS) A boom box is a music player that usually includes a radio and a CD or tape player. In the movie *Kazaam*, the genie lives inside a boom box instead of a lamp.

mischievous (MISS-chuv-vuhss) Someone who is mischievous behaves in an annoying or slightly harmful way. Legends of genies often show them as mischievous or tricky.

supernatural (soo-per-NAT-ur-uhl) Events or things that are supernatural cannot be explained by nature or science. Because genies are said to use magic, they are supernatural creatures.

translator (TRANS-lay-tur) A translator is someone who changes words from one language to another. A French translator made the story *Aladdin and the Wonderful Lamp* famous around the world.

TO LEARN MORE

In the Library

Erickson, Marty. *Fairies*. Mankato, MN: The Child's World, 2022.

Krensky, Stephen. *The Book of Mythical Beasts & Magical Creatures*. New York, NY: DK Publishing, 2020.

Marsico, Katie. *Magic Monsters: From Witches to Goblins*. Minneapolis, MN: Lerner Publications, 2016.

On the Web

Visit our website for links about genies:

childsworld.com/links

Note to Parents, Teachers, and Librarians: We routinely verify our Web links to make sure they are safe and active sites. So encourage your readers to check them out!

INDEX

Aladdin, 4, 11, 16, 21
appearance, 12, 16
archaeology, 4–7

Galland, Antoine, 11

Islam, 9

lamps, 6–7, 11, 15, 16, 19, 21

magazines, 21
movies, 12, 16–18, 21

powers, 8–9, 15, 18–19

television shows, 12, 16, 19, 21
The Thousand and One Nights, 11, 12

wishes, 7, 15, 18–19

ABOUT THE AUTHOR

Rachel Seigel is an avid book enthusiast. She has more than 15 years of experience working with schools and libraries matching books to readers. She is also the author of several nonfiction books for children. When she isn't writing or researching fun facts, Rachel enjoys spending time with her boyfriend and her mischievous dog.